BEGINNING SOLO Guitar

Pop/Rock Classics

T0078805

ISBN 978-1-4803-1284-5

HAL•LEONARD®
CORPORATION
7777 W. BLUEMOUND RD. P.O. BOX 13819 MILWAUKEE, WI 53213

Visit Hal Leonard Online at
www.halleonard.com

Blackbird

Words and Music by John Lennon and Paul McCartney

Intro
Moderately

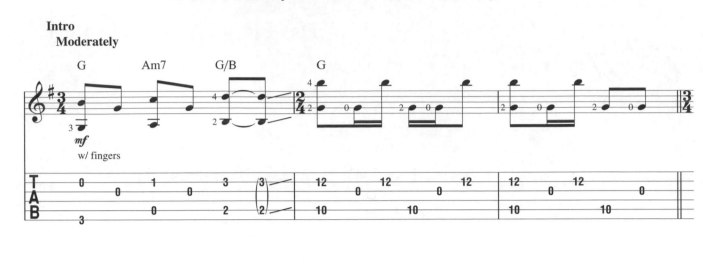

1., 2., 3. Black-bird sing-ing in the dead of night,

1., 3. take these bro-ken wings _____ and learn to fly.
2. take these sunk-en eyes _____ and learn to see.

All your _____ life, _____

you were on—ly wait—ing for this mo—ment 1., 3. to a—rise.
2. to be

To Coda 2 ⊕ **Interlude**

free.

§ Bridge

Black—bird

— fly, —— black—bird ——

— fly —— in—to the

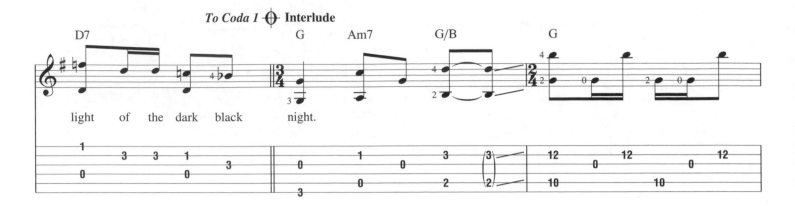

To Coda 1 **Interlude**

light   of   the   dark   black   night.

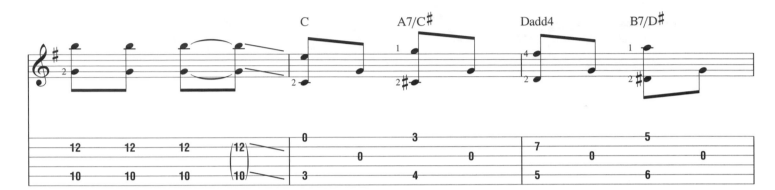

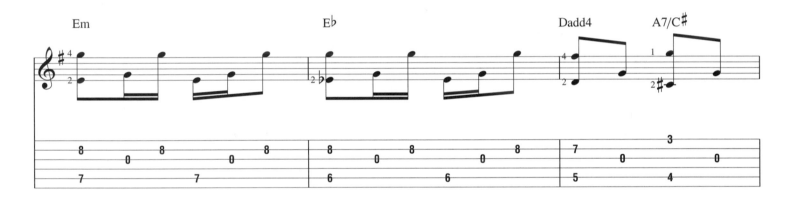

D.S. al Coda 1

Candle in the Wind

Words and Music by Elton John and Bernie Taupin

Intro
Slow, in 2

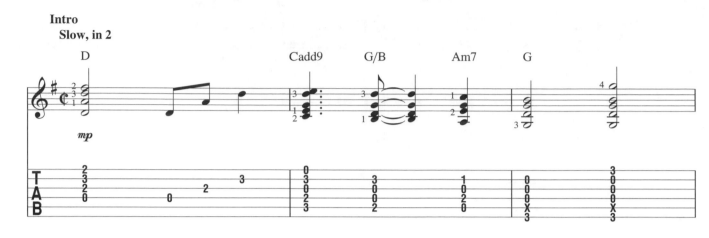

Verse

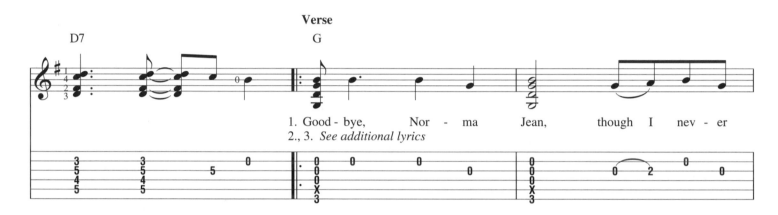

1. Good - bye, Nor - ma Jean, though I nev - er
2., 3. *See additional lyrics*

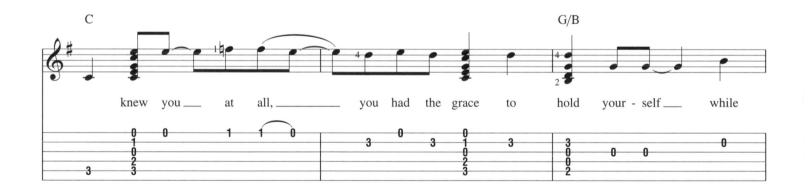

knew you ___ at all, ___ you had the grace to hold your - self ___ while

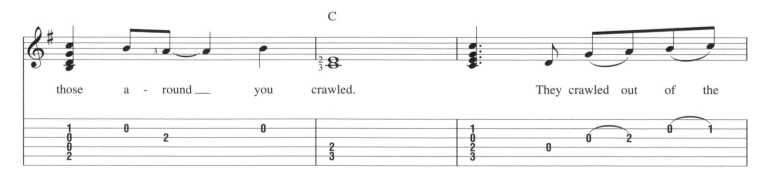

those a - round ___ you crawled. They crawled out of the

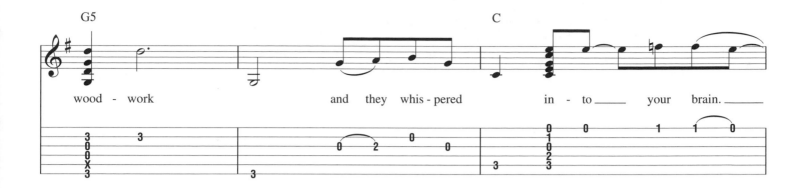

wood - work .... and they whis - pered .... in - to ___ your brain. ___

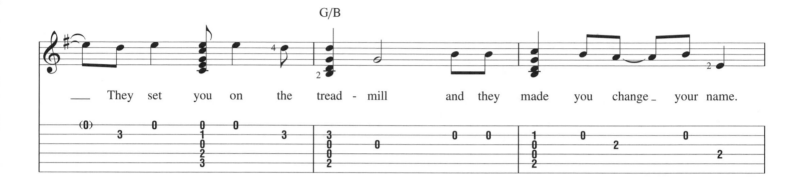

___ They set you on the tread - mill and they made you change_ your name.

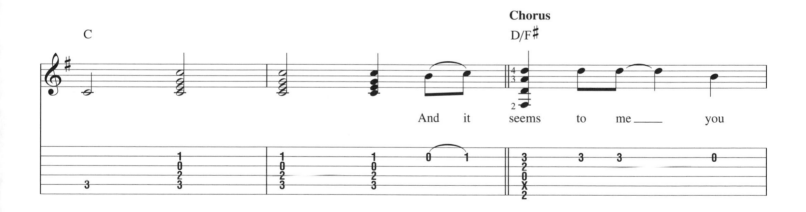

Chorus

And it seems to me ___ you

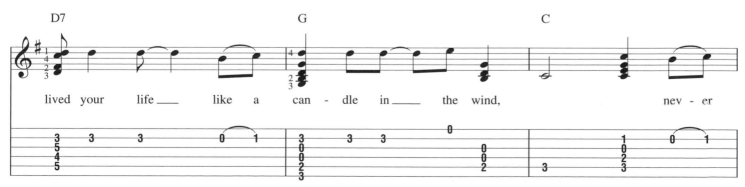

lived your life ___ like a can - dle in ___ the wind, nev - er

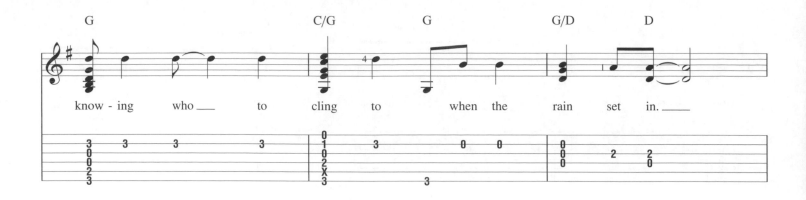

know - ing who ___ to cling to when the rain set in. ___

And I would have liked ___ to know you, but I ___ was

just a kid. ___ Your can - dle burned ___ out long be - fore ___ your

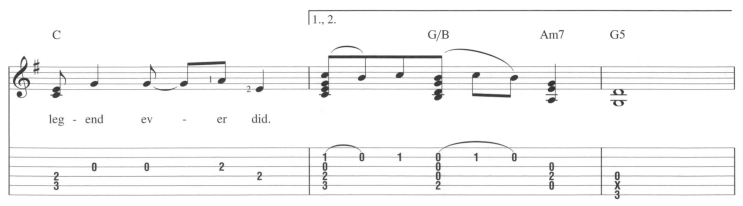

leg - end ev - er did.

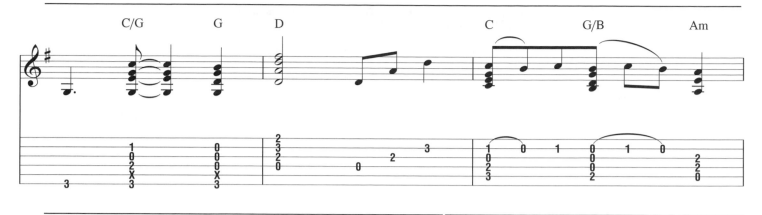

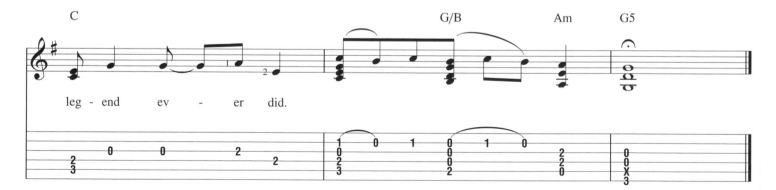

Your can - dle burned _ out long be - fore ___ your

leg - end ev - er did.

Additional Lyrics

2. Loneliness was tough, the toughest role you ever played.
   Hollywood created a superstar and pain was the price you paid.
   And even when you died, oh, the press still hounded you.
   All the papers had to say was that Marilyn was found in the nude.

3. Goodbye, Norma Jean. Though I never knew you at all,
   You had the grace to hold yourself while those around you crawled.
   Goodbye, Norma Jean, from a young man in the twenty-second row,
   Who sees you as something more than sexual, more than just our Marilyn Monroe.

Dust in the Wind

Words and Music by Kerry Livgren

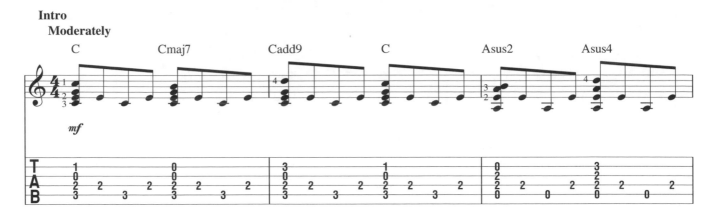

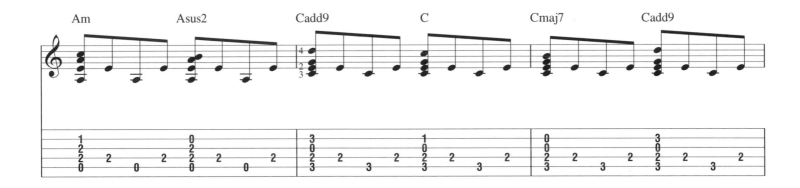

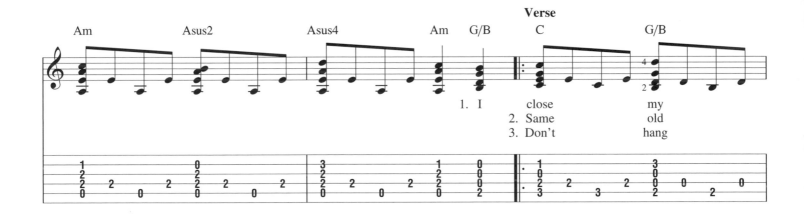

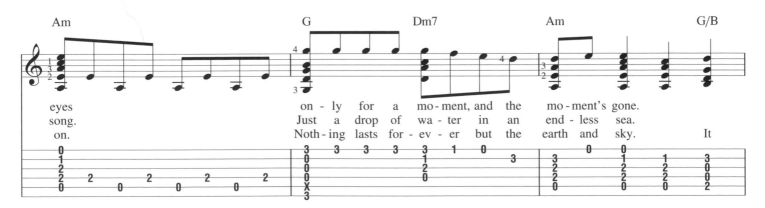

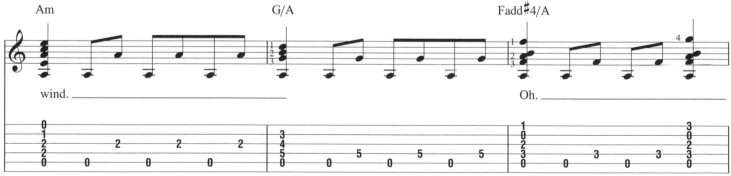

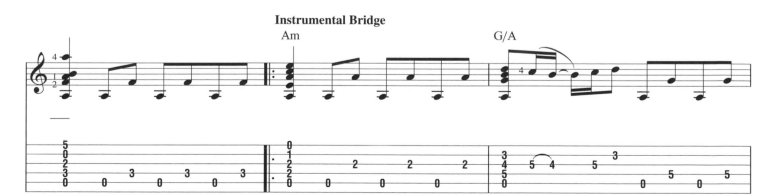

2nd time, D.C. al Coda

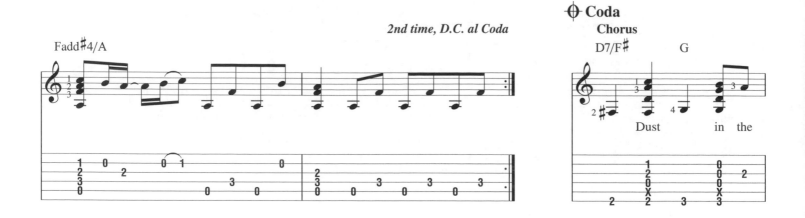

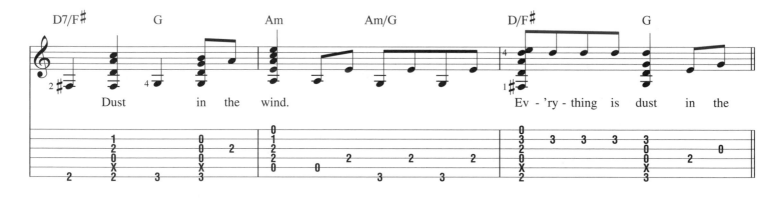

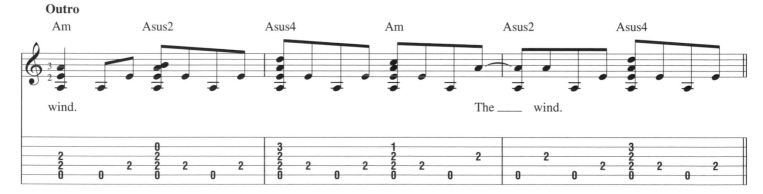

Outro

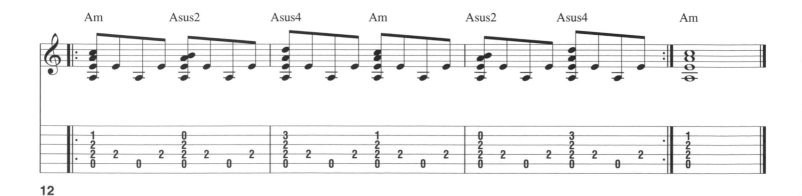

The First Cut Is the Deepest

Words and Music by Cat Stevens

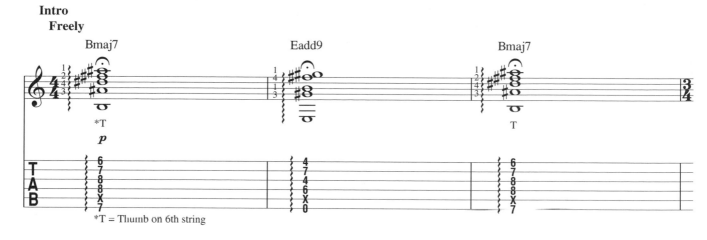

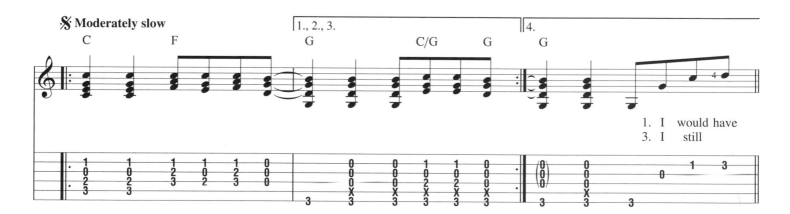

Fields of Gold

Music and Lyrics by Sting

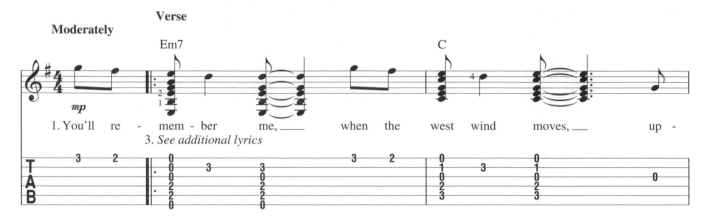

1. You'll re - mem - ber me, when the west wind moves, up -
3. *See additional lyrics*

on the fields of bar - ley. You'll for - get the sun, in his

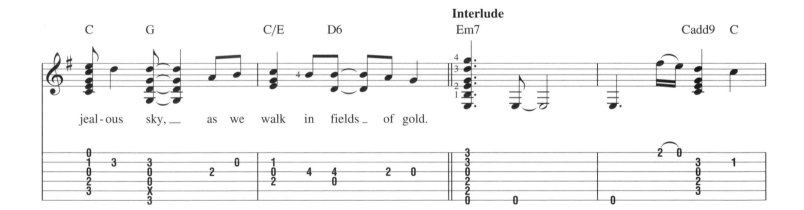

jeal - ous sky, as we walk in fields of gold.

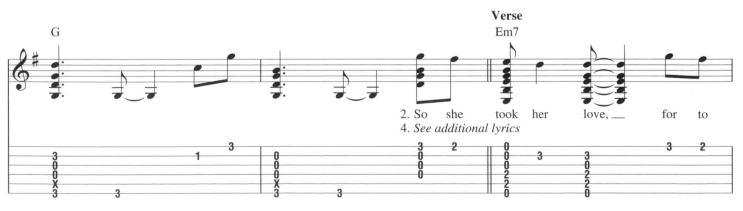

2. So she took her love, for to
4. *See additional lyrics*

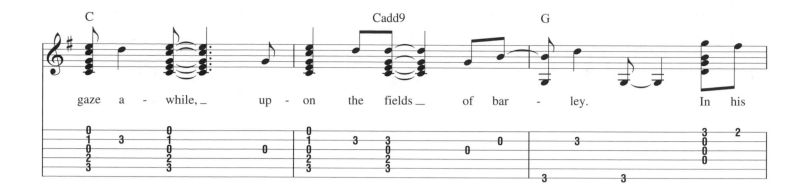

gaze a - while, __ up - on the fields __ of bar - ley. In his

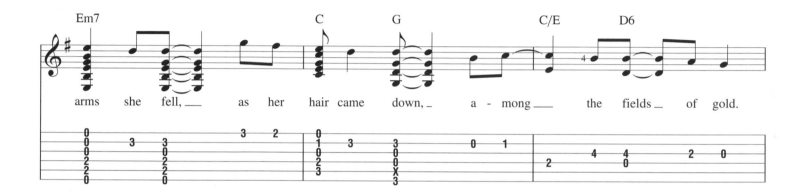

arms she fell, __ as her hair came down, __ a - mong __ the fields __ of gold.

3. Will you

Bridge

I nev - er made

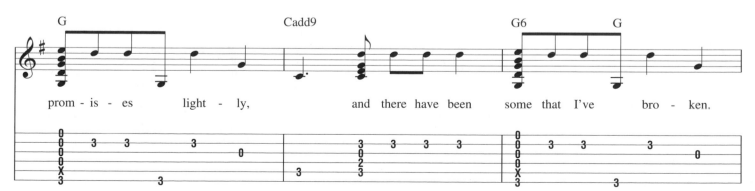

prom - is - es light - ly, and there have been some that I've bro - ken.

But I swear, _ in the days still left, we'll walk _ in fields _ of gold.

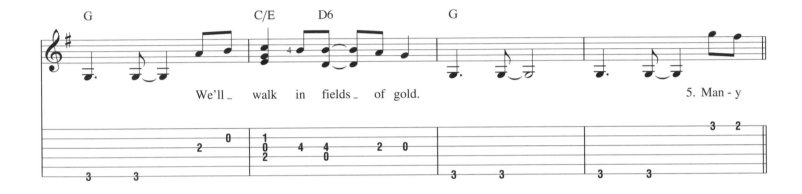

We'll _ walk in fields _ of gold.

5. Man - y

Verse

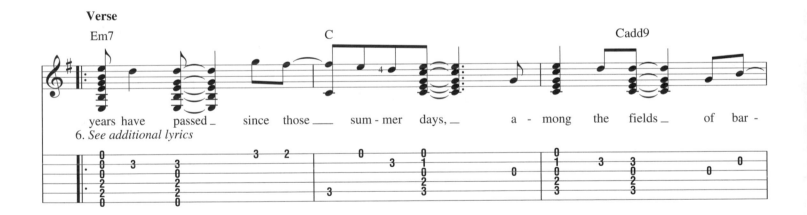

years have passed _ since those _ sum - mer days, _ a - mong the fields _ of bar -

6. *See additional lyrics*

- ley. See the chil - dren run, _ as the sun goes down, _ a - mong _

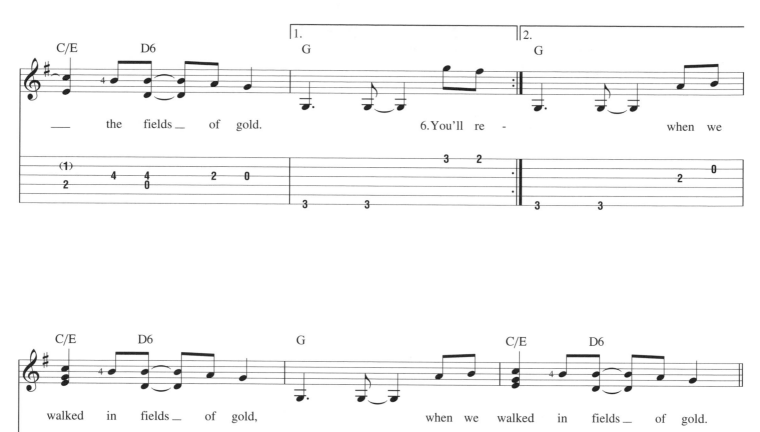

the fields __ of gold.   6. You'll re -   when we

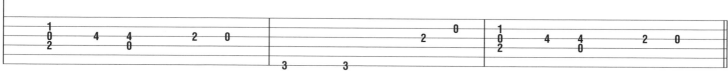

walked   in   fields __ of gold,   when we   walked   in   fields __ of gold.

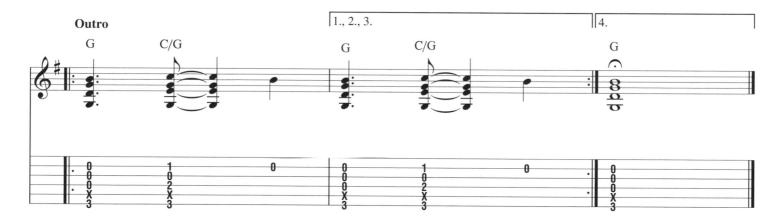

Additional Lyrics

3. Will you stay with me, will you be my love,
   Among the fields of barley?
   We'll forget the sun in his jealous sky,
   As we lie in fields of gold.

4. See the west wind move, like a lover so,
   Upon the fields of barley.
   Feel her body rise, when you kiss her mouth,
   Among the fields of gold.

6. You'll remember me, when the west wind moves,
   Upon the fields of barley.
   You can tell the sun, in his jealous sky,
   When we walked in fields of gold,
   When we walked in fields of gold,
   When we walked in fields of gold.

Free Bird

Words and Music by Allen Collins and Ronnie Van Zant

Intro
Slow

Verse

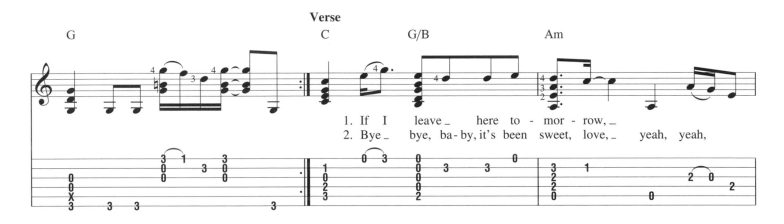

1. If I leave here to-mor-row,
2. Bye bye, ba-by, it's been sweet, love, yeah, yeah,

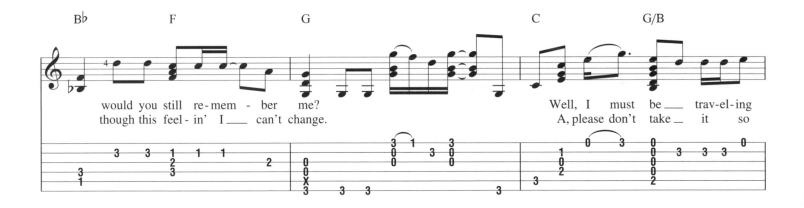

would you still re-mem-ber me?
though this feel-in' I can't change.

Well, I must be trav-el-ing
A, please don't take it so

on now,
bad-ly,

'cause there's too man-y plac-es I've got to see.
'cause Lord knows I'm to blame.

Goodbye Yellow Brick Road

Words and Music by Elton John and Bernie Taupin

Intro
Slowly, in 2

Verse

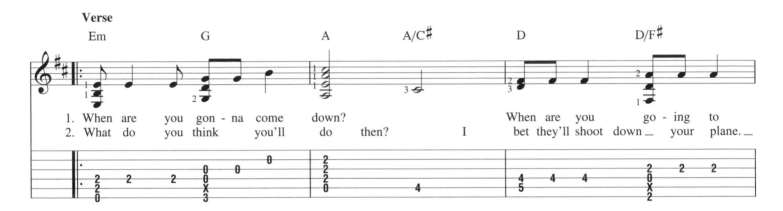

1. When are you gon-na come down? When are you go-ing to
2. What do you think you'll do then? I bet they'll shoot down __ your plane. __

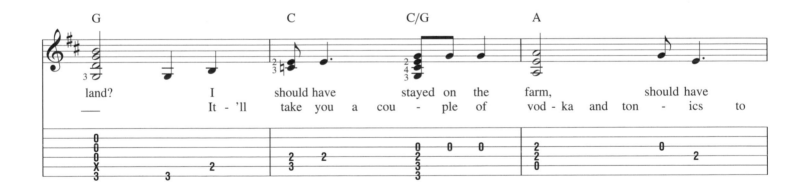

land? I should have stayed on the farm, should have
__ It-'ll take you a cou - ple of vod-ka and ton-ics to

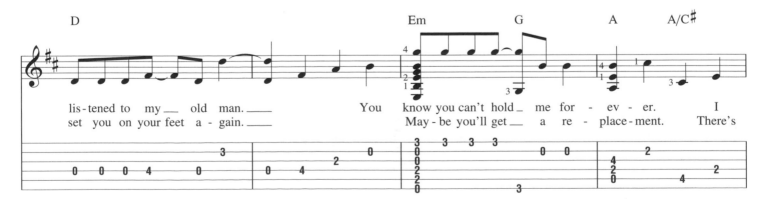

lis-tened to my __ old man. __ You know you can't hold __ me for-ev-er. I
set you on your feet a-gain. __ May-be you'll get __ a re-place-ment. There's

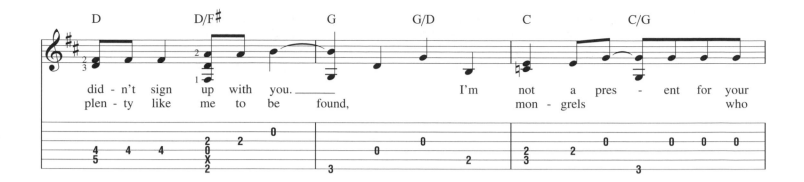

did - n't sign up with you. _____ I'm not a pres - ent for your
plen - ty like me to be found, mon - grels who

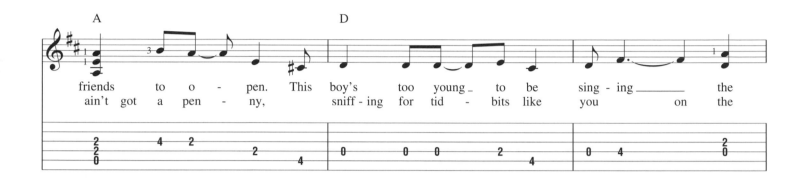

friends to o - pen. This boy's too young _____ to be sing - ing _____ the
ain't got a pen - ny, sniff - ing for tid - bits like you on the

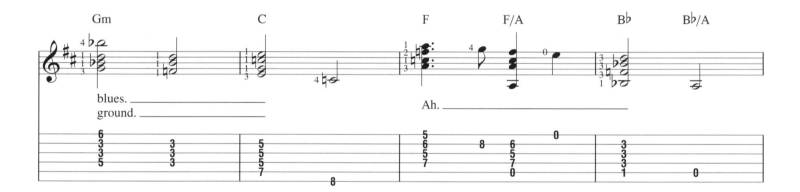

blues. _____
ground. _____

Ah. _____

Chorus

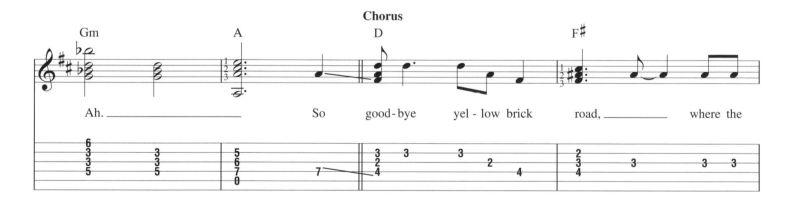

Ah. _____

So good-bye yel - low brick road, _____ where the

dogs of so - ci - e - ty howl. You can't plant me in your pent - house. I'm

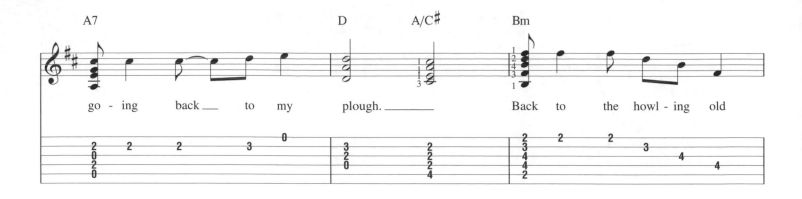

go - ing back ___ to my plough. _____ Back to the howl - ing old

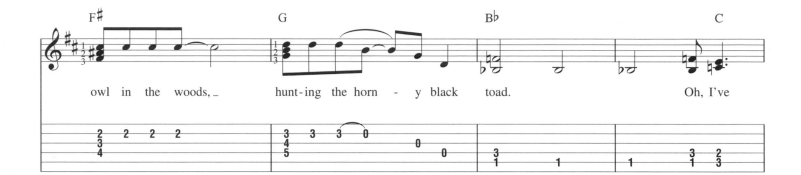

owl in the woods, _ hunt-ing the horn - y black toad. Oh, I've

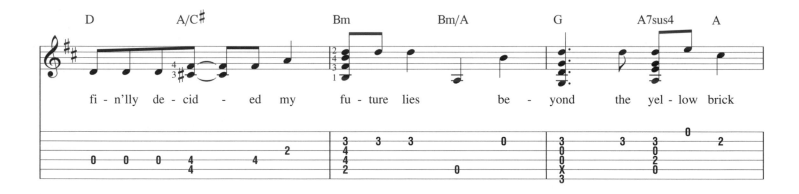

fi - n'lly de - cid - ed my fu - ture lies be - yond the yel - low brick

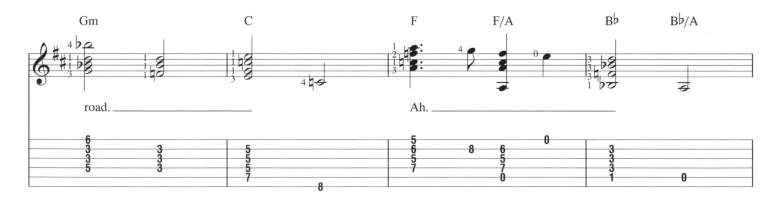

road. _____ Ah. _____

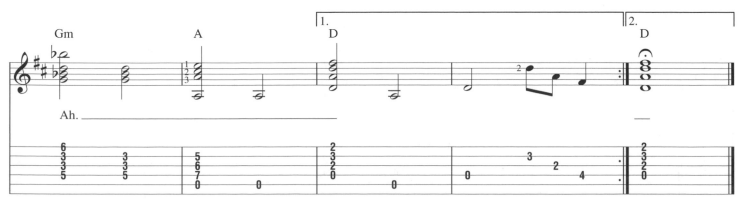

Ah. _____ _____

Man in the Mirror

Words and Music by Glen Ballard and Siedah Garrett

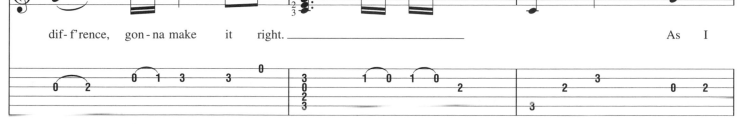

Pre-Chorus

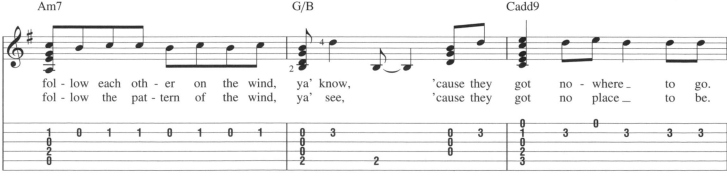

Moondance

Words and Music by Van Morrison

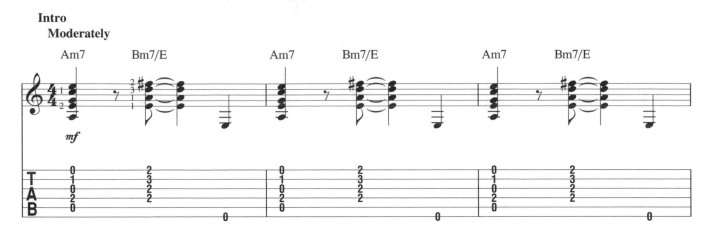

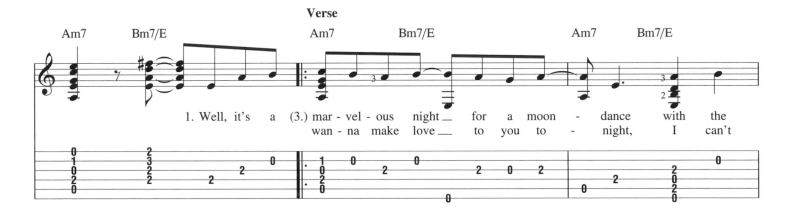

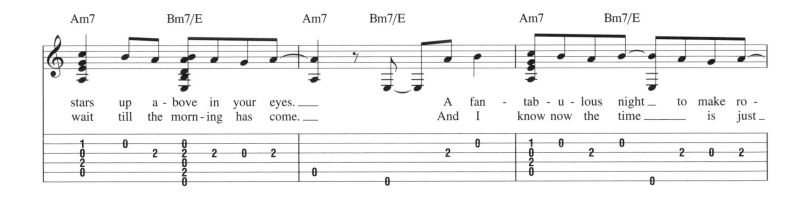

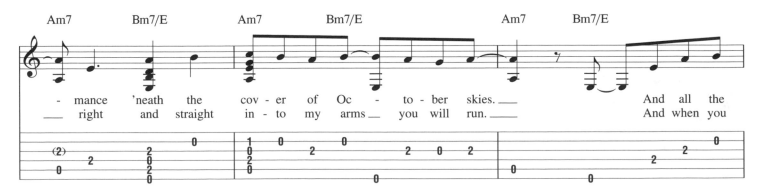

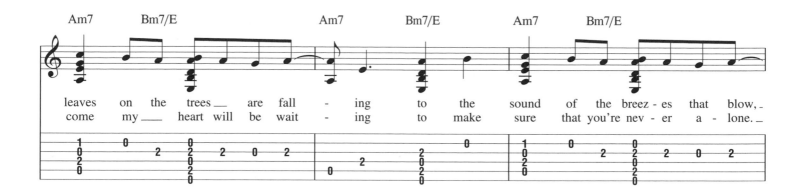

leaves on the trees are fall - ing to the sound of the breez - es that blow,
come my heart will be wait - ing to make sure that you're nev - er a - lone.

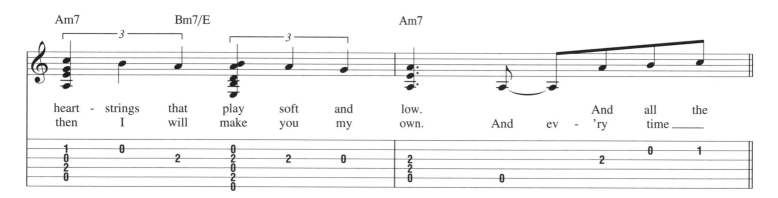

and I'm try - ing to please to the call - ing of your
There and then all my dreams will come true, dear, of there and

heart - strings that play soft and low. And all the
then I will make you my own. And ev - 'ry time

Pre-Chorus

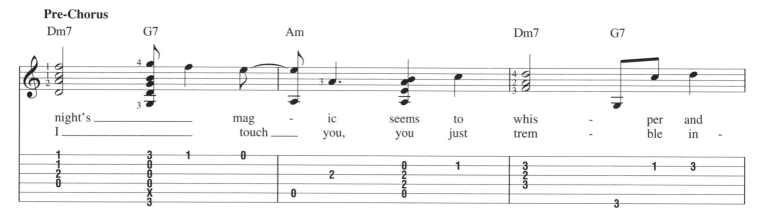

night's mag - ic seems to whis - per and
I touch you, you just trem - ble in -

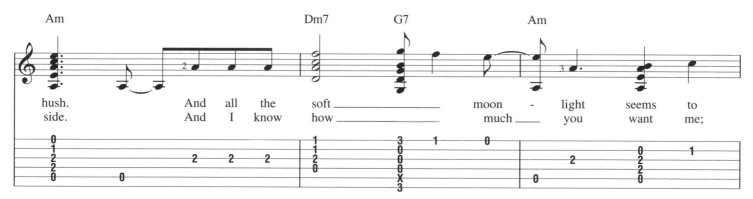

hush. And all the soft moon - light seems to
side. And I know how much you want me;

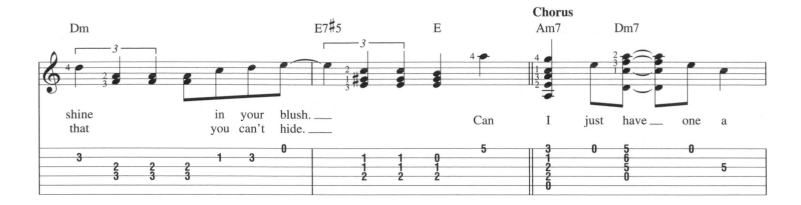

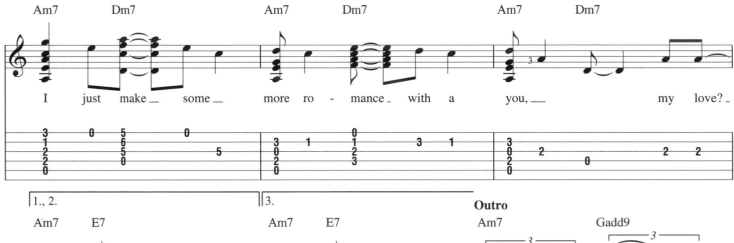

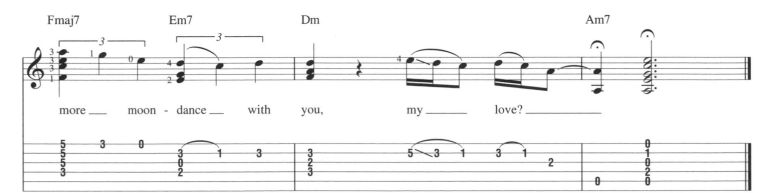

More Than Words

Words and Music by Nuno Bettencourt and Gary Cherone

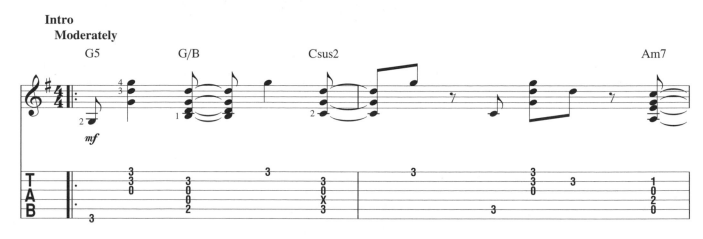

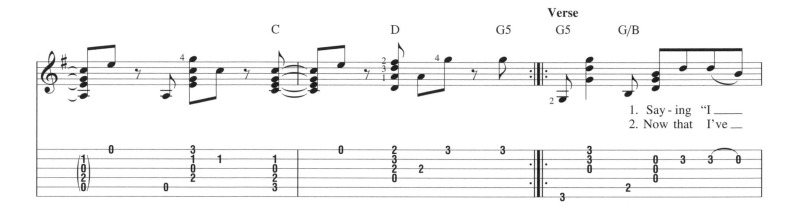

1. Say - ing "I _____
2. Now that I've _____

love _____ you," is not the words _____ I want to hear _____ from
tried _____ to talk to you _____ and make you un - der -

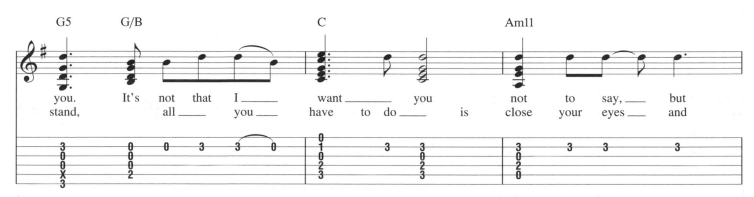

you. It's not that I _____ want _____ you not to say, _____ but
stand, all _____ you _____ have to do _____ is close your eyes _____ and

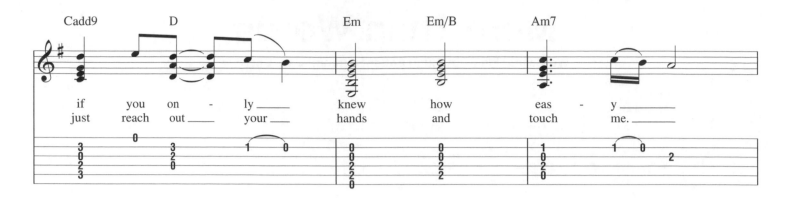

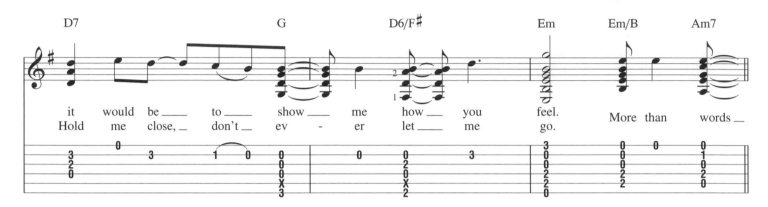

Chorus

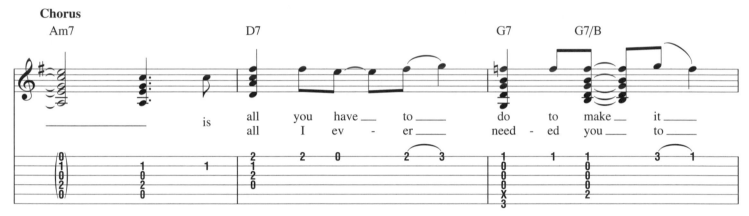

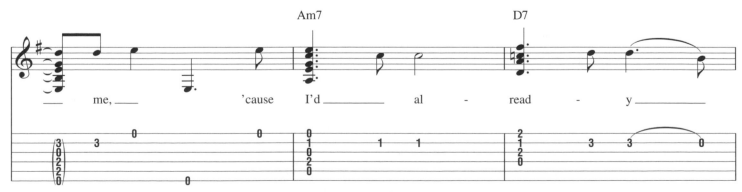

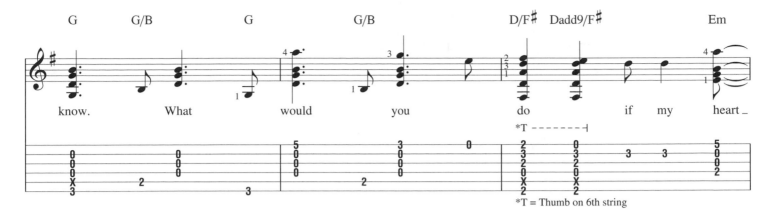

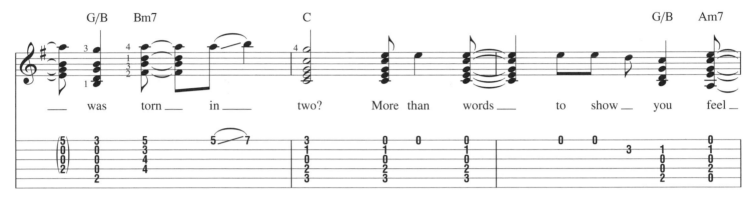

*T = Thumb on 6th string

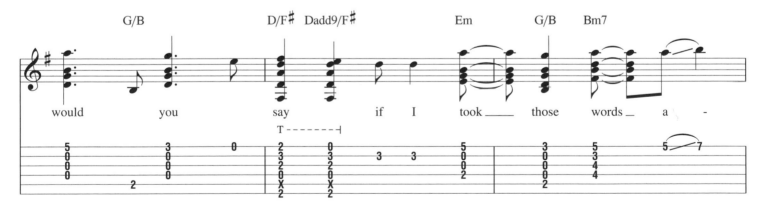

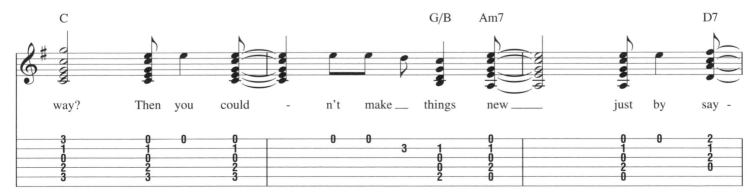

Interlude

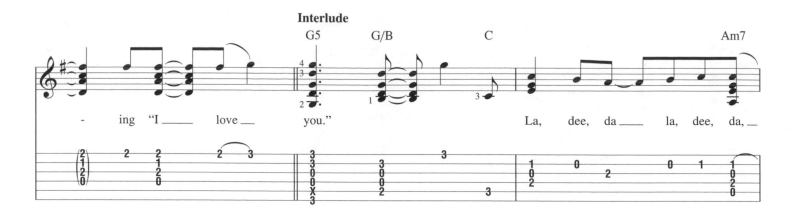

- ing "I ___ love ___ you." La, dee, da ___ la, dee, da, ___

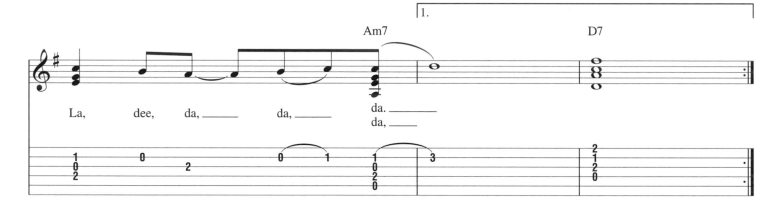

___ dee, da, ___ da, ___ da. More ___ than ___ words.

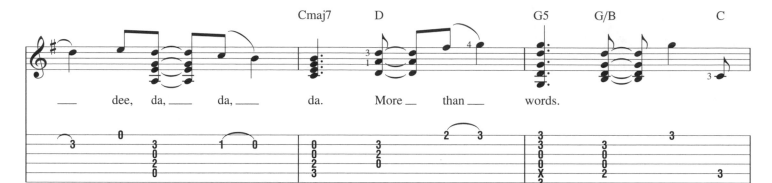

1.

La, dee, da, ___ da, ___ da. ___
da, ___

2.

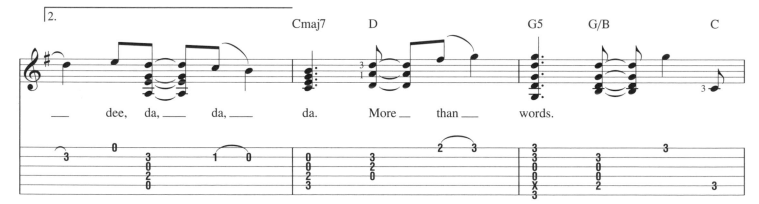

___ dee, da, ___ da, ___ da. More ___ than ___ words.

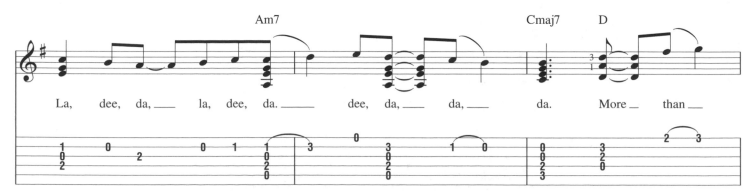

La, dee, da, ___ la, dee, da. ___ dee, da, ___ da, ___ da. More ___ than ___

words.   La, dee, da,___ la, dee, da._____   La,___

Outro

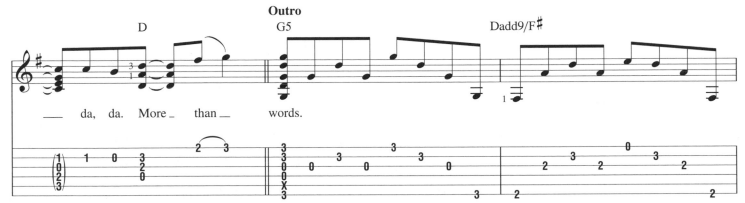

___ da, da. More ___ than ___ words.

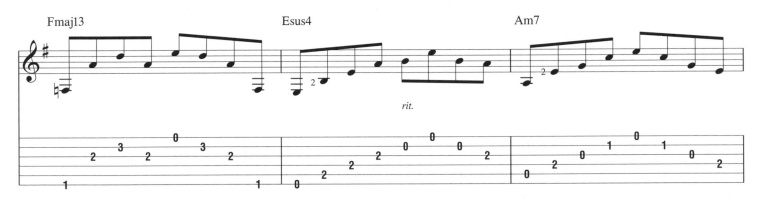

Slower

More   than ___ words.

Freely

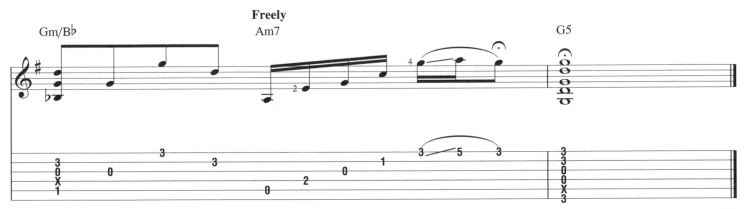

She's Always a Woman

Words and Music by Billy Joel

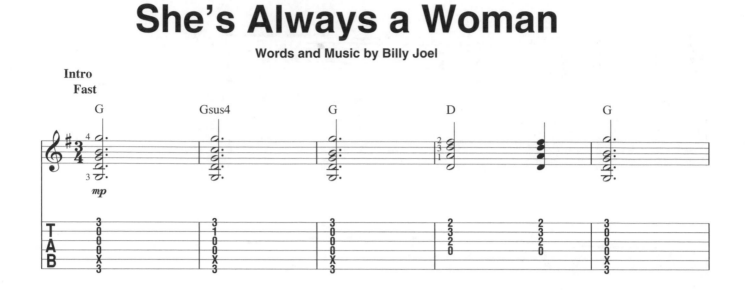

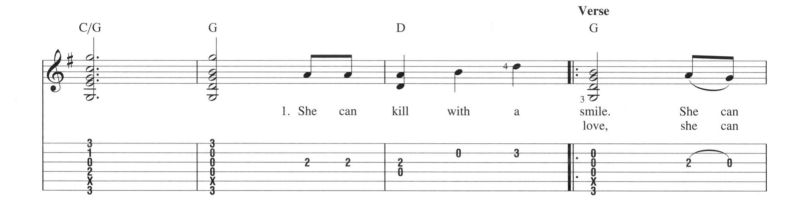

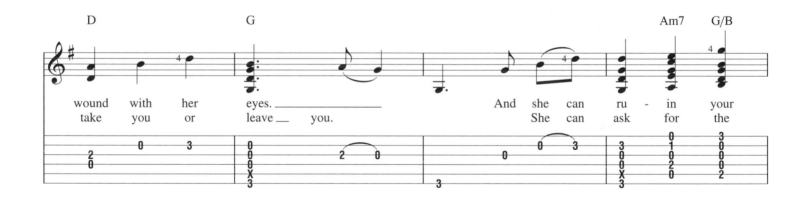

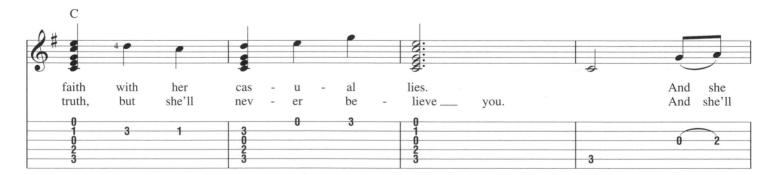

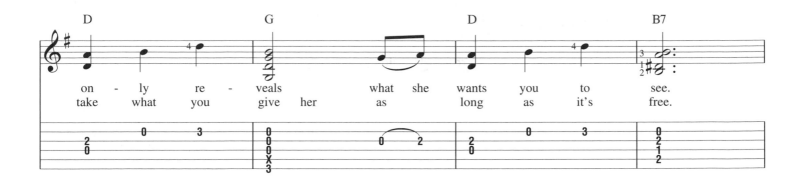

only reveals what she wants you to see.
take what you give her as long as it's free.

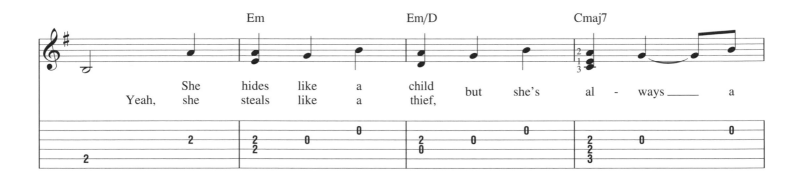

Yeah, she hides like a child but she's al - ways _____ a
she steals like a thief,

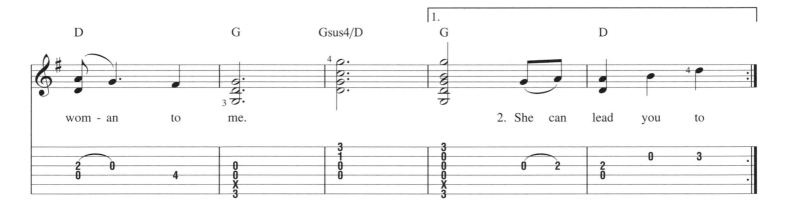

wom - an to me. 2. She can lead you to

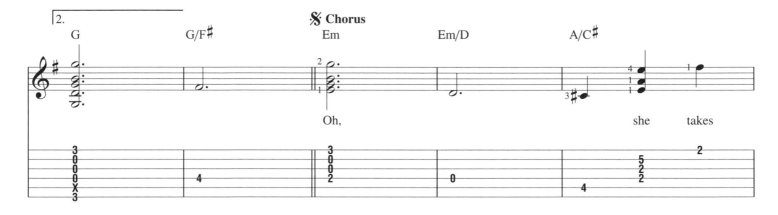

Chorus

Oh, she takes

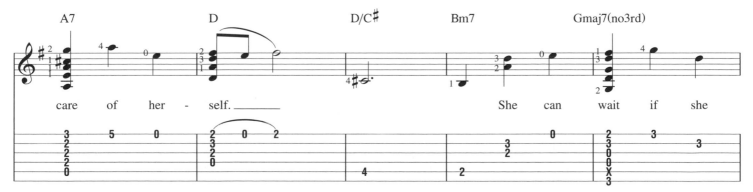

care of her - self. _____ She can wait if she

wants, she's a - head of her time.

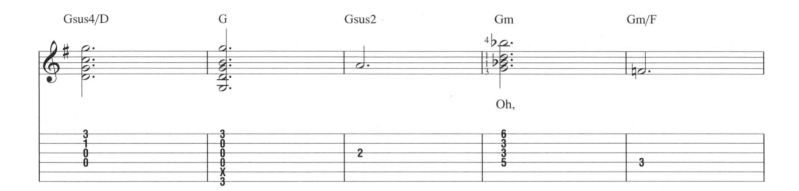

Oh,

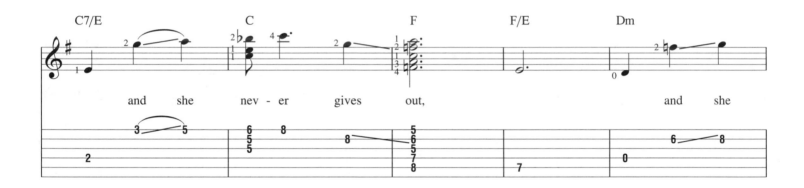

and she nev - er gives out, and she

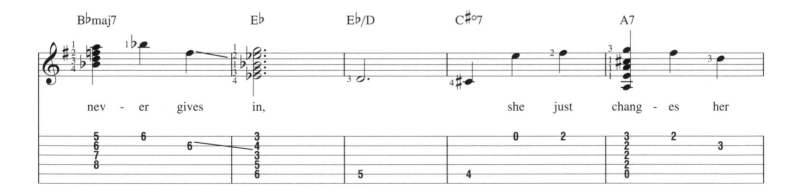

nev - er gives in, she just chang - es her

mind.

3. And she'll prom - ise you
4. She is fre - quent - ly

Verse

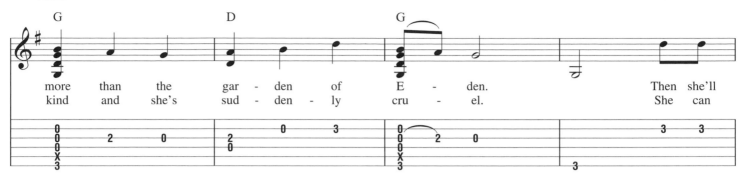

more than the gar - den of E - den. Then she'll
kind and she's sud - den - ly cru - el. She can

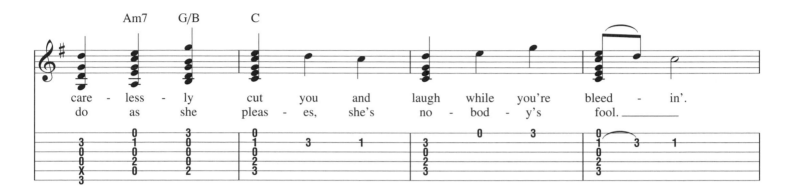

care - less - ly cut you and laugh while you're bleed - in'.
do as she pleas - es, she's no - bod - y's fool. _____

To Coda 1 ⊕

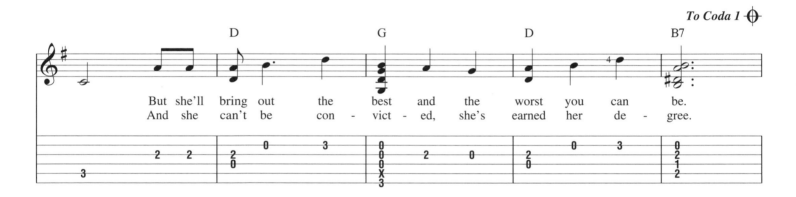

But she'll bring out the best and the worst you can be.
And she can't be con - vict - ed, she's earned her de - gree.

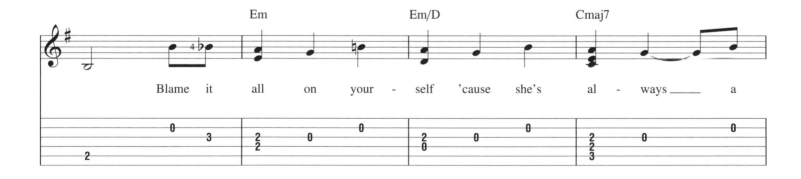

Blame it all on your - self 'cause she's al - ways _____ a

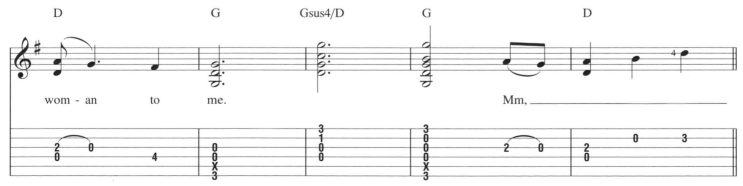

wom - an to me. Mm, _____

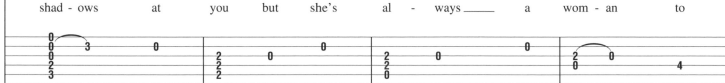

Tears in Heaven

Words and Music by Eric Clapton and Will Jennings

Intro
Moderately slow

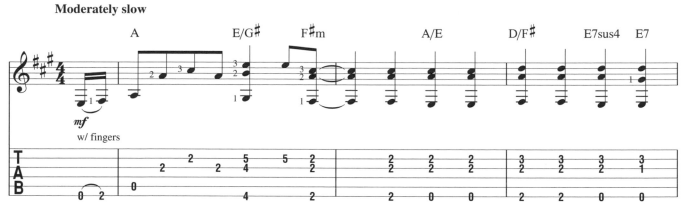

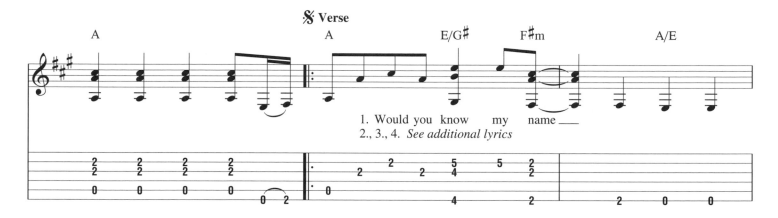

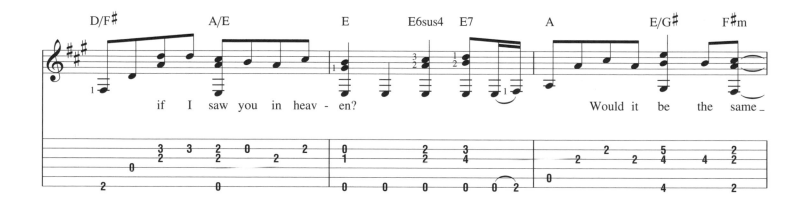

I must be strong ___ and car - ry on ___

'cause I know I don't be - long here in heav -

4th time, To Coda ⊕

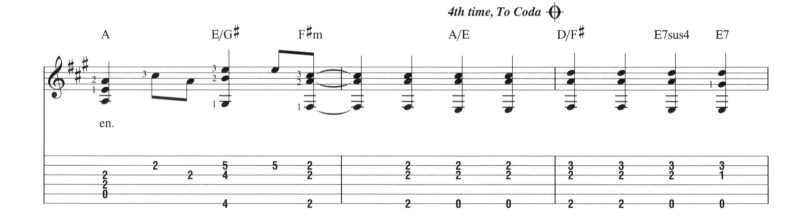

en.

1.

2.

Bridge

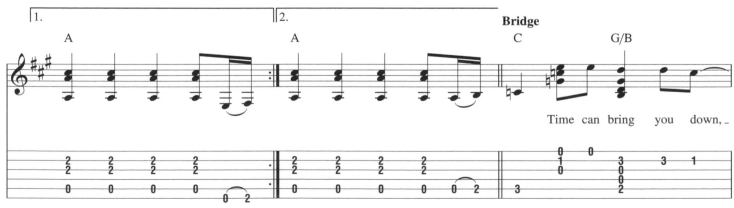

Time can bring you down, ___

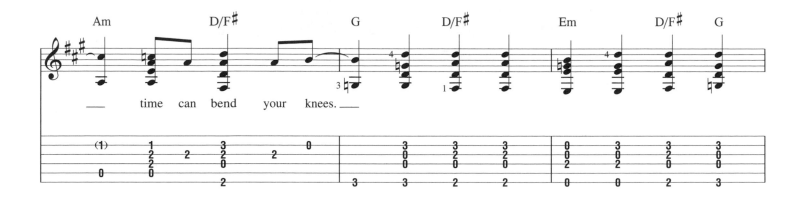

time can bend your knees. ___

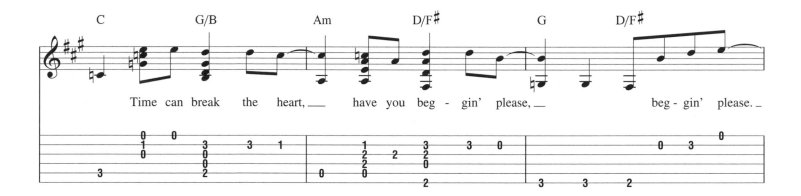

Time can break the heart, ___ have you beg - gin' please, ___ beg - gin' please. _

D.S. al Coda
(take repeat)

⊕ **Coda**

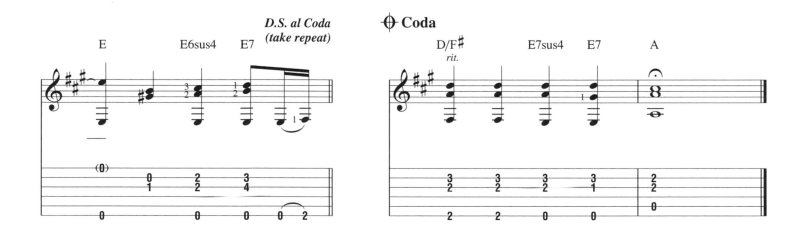

Additional Lyrics

2. Would you hold my hand if I saw you in heaven?
   Would you help me stand if I saw you in heaven?
   I'll find my way through night and day
   'Cause I know I just can't stay here in heaven.

3. *Instrumental*
   Beyond the door there's peace, I'm sure,
   And I know there'll be no more tears in heaven.

4. Would you know my name if I saw you in heaven?
   Would you be the same if I saw you in heaven?
   I must be strong and carry on
   'Cause I know I don't belong here in heaven.

The Sound of Silence

Words and Music by Paul Simon

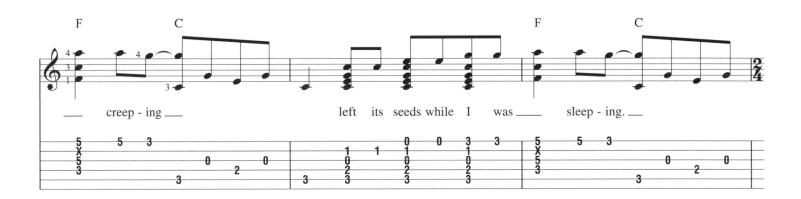

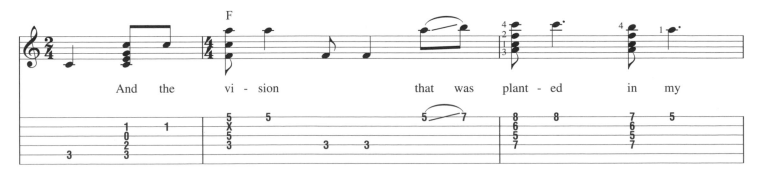

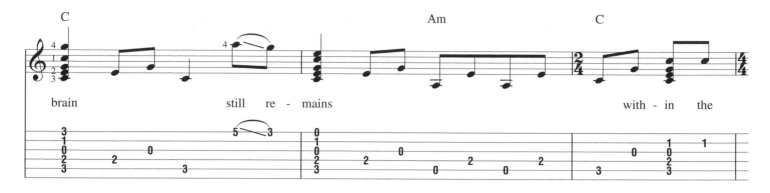

brain   still   re - mains   with - in   the

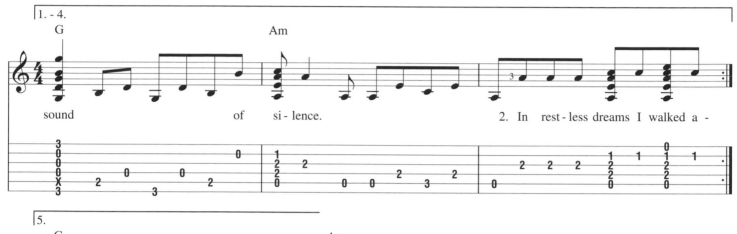

sound   of   si - lence.   2. In   rest - less dreams I walked a -

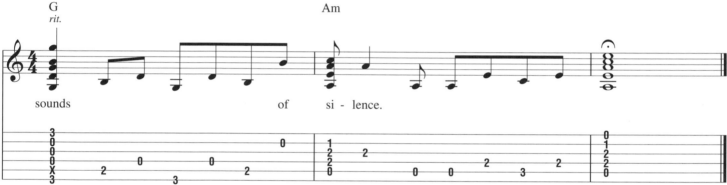

sounds   of   si - lence.

Additional Lyrics

2. In restless dreams I walked alone,
   Narrow streets of cobblestone.
   'Neath the halo of a street lamp,
   I turned my collar to the cold and damp
   When my eyes were stabbed by the flash of a neon light
   That split the night
   And touched the sound of silence.

3. And in the naked light I saw
   Ten thousand people, maybe more.
   People talking without speaking,
   People hearing without list'ning.
   People writing songs that voices never shared
   And no one dared
   Disturb the sound of silence.

4. "Fools!" said I, "You do not know,
   Silence like a cancer grows.
   Hear my words that I might teach you.
   Take my arms that I might reach you."
   But my words like silent raindrops fell,
   And echoed in wells of silence.

5. And the people bowed and prayed
   To the neon god they made.
   And the sign flashed out its warning
   In the words that it was forming.
   And the sign said the words of the prophets are written on the subway walls
   And tenement halls,
   And whispered in the sounds of silence.

You're the Inspiration

Words and Music by Peter Cetera and David Foster

Intro
Slow, in 2

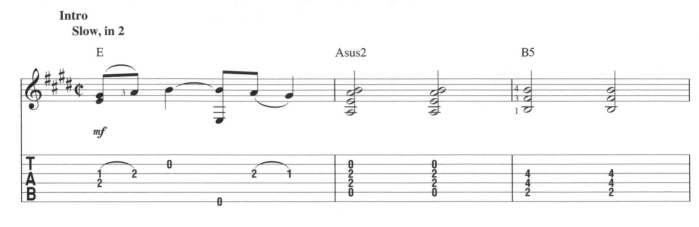

Verse

1. You know our love was meant to be
(2.) know, yes I know that it's plain to see

the kind of love that lasts __ for - ev - er. _____
we're so in love when we're to - geth - er. _____ Now I

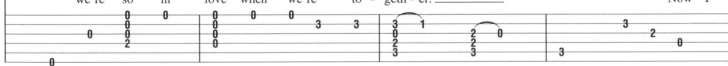

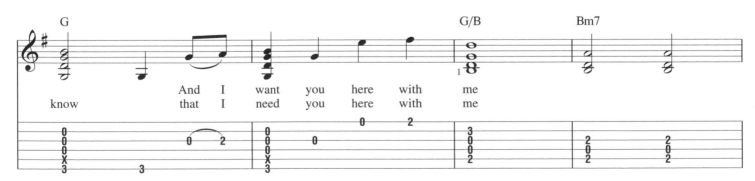

And I want you here with me
know that I need you here with me

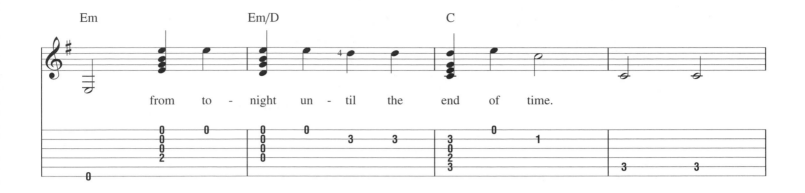

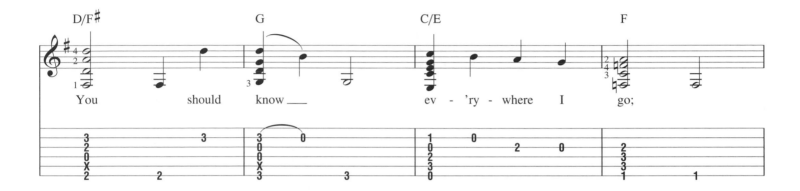

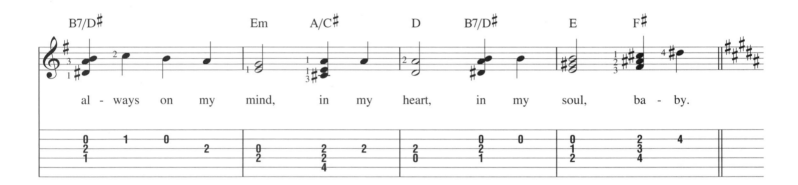

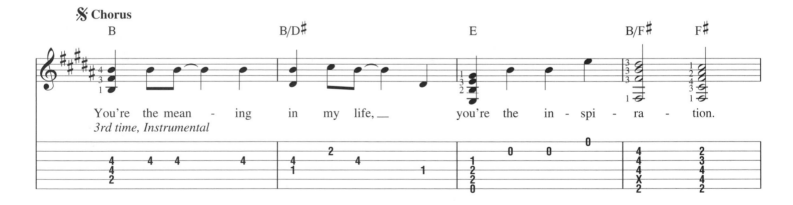

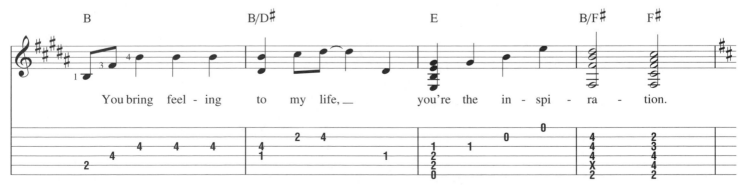

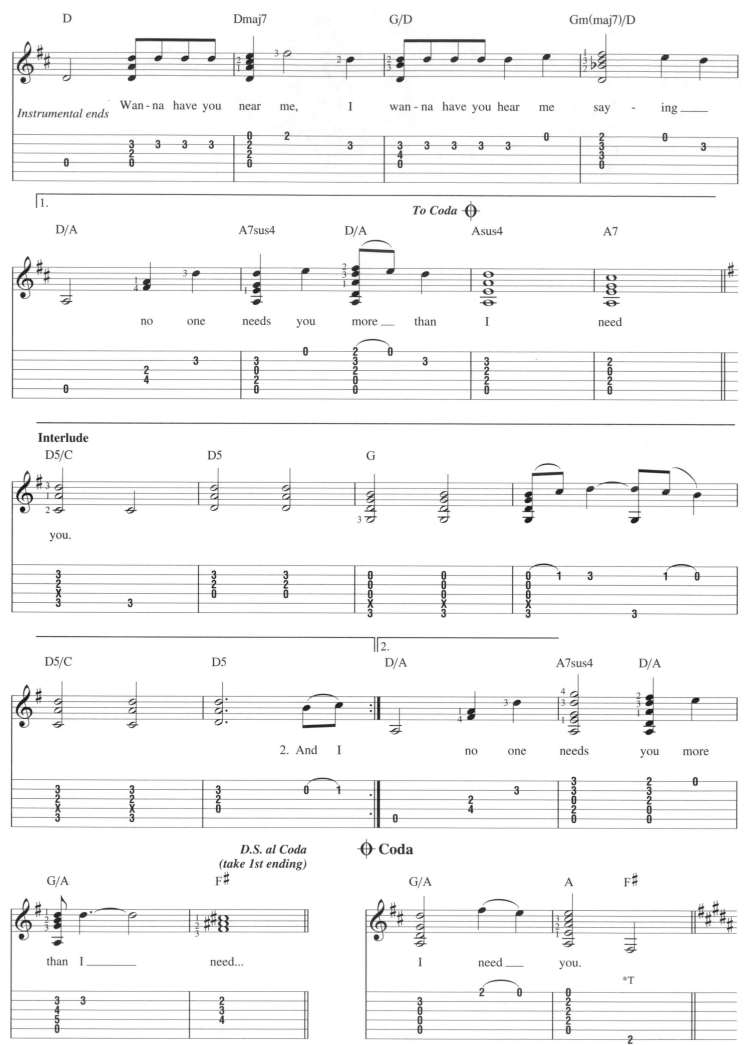

When a Man Loves a Woman

Words and Music by Calvin Lewis and Andrew Wright

Intro
Slow, in 2

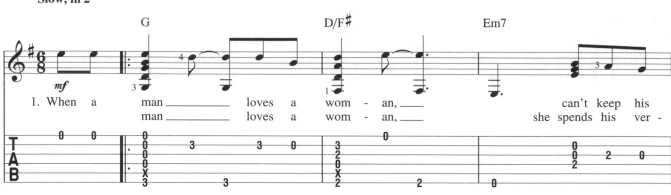

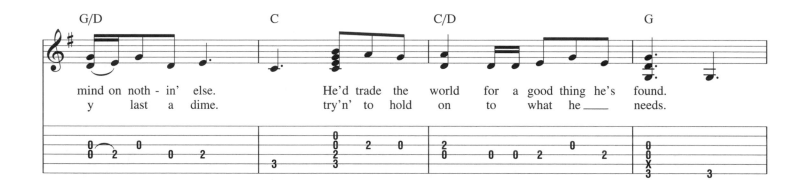

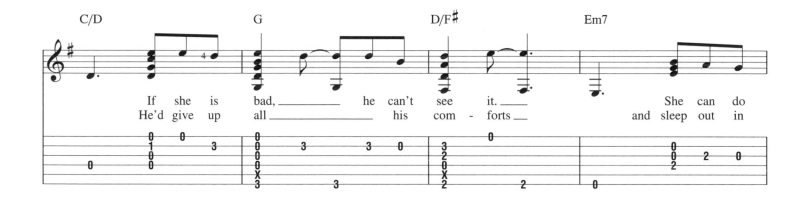

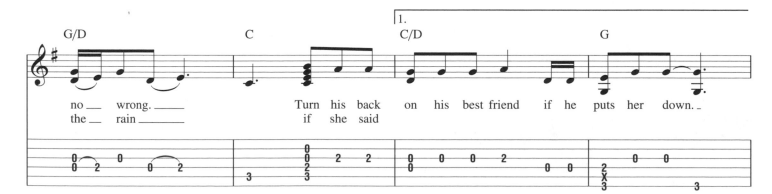

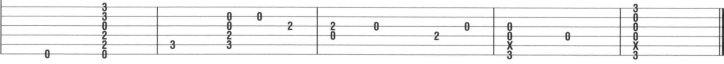

FINGERPICKING GUITAR BOOKS

Hone your fingerpicking skills with these great songbooks featuring solo guitar arrangements in standard notation and tablature. The arrangements in these books are carefully written for intermediate-level guitarists. Each song combines melody and harmony in one superb guitar fingerpicking arrangement. Each book also includes an introduction to basic fingerstyle guitar.

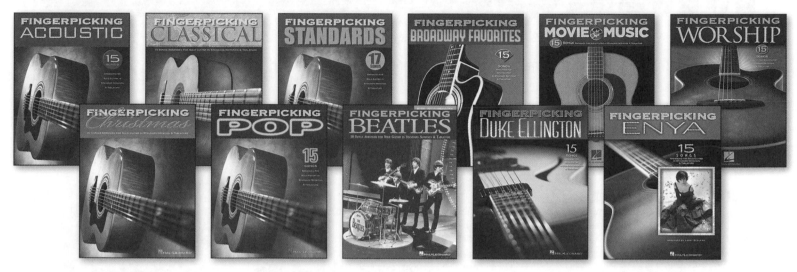

FINGERPICKING ACOUSTIC
00699614...$10.99

FINGERPICKING ACOUSTIC ROCK
00699764...$9.99

FINGERPICKING BACH
00699793...$8.95

FINGERPICKING BALLADS
00699717...$9.99

FINGERPICKING BEATLES
00699049...$19.99

FINGERPICKING BEETHOVEN
00702390...$7.99

FINGERPICKING BLUES
00701277 ....$7.99

FINGERPICKING BROADWAY FAVORITES
00699843...$9.99

FINGERPICKING BROADWAY HITS
00699838...$7.99

FINGERPICKING CELTIC FOLK
00701148...$7.99

FINGERPICKING CHILDREN'S SONGS
00699712...$9.99

FINGERPICKING CHRISTIAN
00701076 ....$7.99

FINGERPICKING CHRISTMAS
00699599...$8.95

FINGERPICKING CHRISTMAS CLASSICS
00701695...$7.99

FINGERPICKING CLASSICAL
00699620...$8.95

FINGERPICKING COUNTRY
00699687...$9.99

FINGERPICKING DISNEY
00699711...$10.99

FINGERPICKING DUKE ELLINGTON
00699845...$9.99

FINGERPICKING ENYA
00701161...$9.99

FINGERPICKING GOSPEL
00701059...$7.99

FINGERPICKING GUITAR BIBLE
00691040 ....$19.99

FINGERPICKING HYMNS
00699688...$8.95

FINGERPICKING IRISH SONGS
00701965...$7.99

FINGERPICKING JAZZ STANDARDS
00699840...$7.99

FINGERPICKING LATIN STANDARDS
00699837...$7.99

FINGERPICKING ANDREW LLOYD WEBBER
00699839...$9.99

FINGERPICKING LOVE SONGS
00699841...$9.99

FINGERPICKING LOVE STANDARDS
00699836 ....$9.99

FINGERPICKING LULLABYES
00701276...$9.99

FINGERPICKING MOVIE MUSIC
00699919...$9.99

FINGERPICKING MOZART
00699794...$8.95

FINGERPICKING POP
00699615...$9.99

FINGERPICKING PRAISE
00699714...$8.95

FINGERPICKING ROCK
00699716...$9.99

FINGERPICKING STANDARDS
00699613...$9.99

FINGERPICKING WEDDING
00699637...$9.99

FINGERPICKING WORSHIP
00700554...$7.99

**FINGERPICKING NEIL YOUNG –
GREATEST HITS**
00700134...$12.99

FINGERPICKING YULETIDE
00699654...$9.99

HAL•LEONARD®
CORPORATION

7777 W. BLUEMOUND RD. P.O. BOX 13819 MILWAUKEE, WI 53213

Visit Hal Leonard online at **www.halleonard.com**

Prices, contents and availability subject to change without notice.

0113

JAZZ GUITAR CHORD MELODY SOLOS

This series features chord melody arrangements in standard notation and tablature of songs for intermediate guitarists.

ALL-TIME STANDARDS **INCLUDES TAB**
27 songs, including: All of Me • Bewitched • Come Fly with Me • A Fine Romance • Georgia on My Mind • How High the Moon • I'll Never Smile Again • I've Got You Under My Skin • It's De-Lovely • It's Only a Paper Moon • My Romance • Satin Doll • The Surrey with the Fringe on Top • Yesterdays • and more.
00699757 Solo Guitar $14.99

CHRISTMAS CAROLS **INCLUDES TAB**
26 songs, including: Auld Lang Syne • Away in a Manger • Deck the Hall • God Rest Ye Merry, Gentlemen • Good King Wenceslas • Here We Come A-Wassailing • It Came upon the Midnight Clear • Joy to the World • O Holy Night • O Little Town of Bethlehem • Silent Night • Toyland • We Three Kings of Orient Are • and more.
00701697 Solo Guitar $12.99

DISNEY SONGS **INCLUDES TAB**
27 songs, including: Beauty and the Beast • Can You Feel the Love Tonight • Candle on the Water • Colors of the Wind • A Dream Is a Wish Your Heart Makes • Heigh-Ho • Some Day My Prince Will Come • Under the Sea • When You Wish upon a Star • A Whole New World (Aladdin's Theme) • Zip-A-Dee-Doo-Dah • and more.
00701902 Solo Guitar $14.99

DUKE ELLINGTON **INCLUDES TAB**
25 songs, including: C-Jam Blues • Caravan • Do Nothin' Till You Hear from Me • Don't Get Around Much Anymore • I Got It Bad and That Ain't Good • I'm Just a Lucky So and So • In a Sentimental Mood • It Don't Mean a Thing (If It Ain't Got That Swing) • Mood Indigo • Perdido • Prelude to a Kiss • Satin Doll • and more.
00700636 Solo Guitar $12.99

FAVORITE STANDARDS **INCLUDES TAB**
27 songs, including: All the Way • Autumn in New York • Blue Skies • Cheek to Cheek • Don't Get Around Much Anymore • How Deep Is the Ocean • I'll Be Seeing You • Isn't It Romantic? • It Could Happen to You • The Lady Is a Tramp • Moon River • Speak Low • Take the "A" Train • Willow Weep for Me • Witchcraft • and more.
00699756 Solo Guitar $14.99

FINGERPICKING JAZZ STANDARDS **INCLUDES TAB**
15 songs: Autumn in New York • Body and Soul • Can't Help Lovin' Dat Man • Easy Living • A Fine Romance • Have You Met Miss Jones? • I'm Beginning to See the Light • It Could Happen to You • My Romance • Stella by Starlight • Tangerine • The Very Thought of You • The Way You Look Tonight • When Sunny Gets Blue • Yesterdays.
00699840 Solo Guitar $7.99

JAZZ BALLADS **INCLUDES TAB**
27 songs, including: Body and Soul • Darn That Dream • Easy to Love (You'd Be So Easy to Love) • Here's That Rainy Day • In a Sentimental Mood • Misty • My Foolish Heart • My Funny Valentine • The Nearness of You • Stella by Starlight • Time After Time • The Way You Look Tonight • When Sunny Gets Blue • and more.
00699755 Solo Guitar $14.99

JAZZ CLASSICS **INCLUDES TAB**
27 songs, including: Blue in Green • Bluesette • Bouncing with Bud • Cast Your Fate to the Wind • Con Alma • Doxy • Epistrophy • Footprints • Giant Steps • Invitation • Lullaby of Birdland • Lush Life • A Night in Tunisia • Nuages • Ruby, My Dear • St. Thomas • Stolen Moments • Waltz for Debby • Yardbird Suite • and more.
00699758 Solo Guitar $14.99

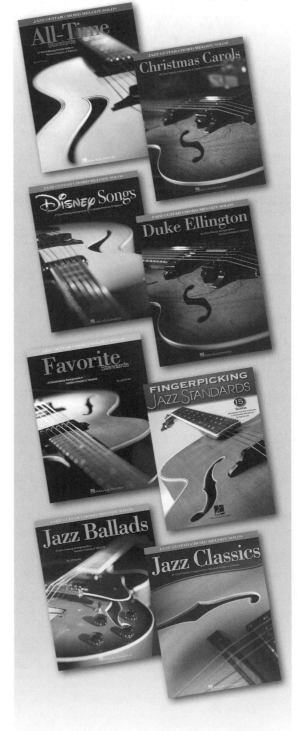

"Well-crafted arrangements that sound great and are still accessible to most players."
— *Guitar Edge* magazine

HAL•LEONARD®
www.halleonard.com